My Mother Is a Doctor

Written by Charnan Simon • Illustrated by Patrick Girouard

Published in the United States of America by The Child's World®
PO Box 326 • Chanhassen, MN 55317-0326
800-599-READ • www.childsworld.com

Reading Adviser

Cecilia Minden-Cupp, PhD, Former Language and Literacy Program Director,
Harvard Graduate School of Education, Cambridge, Massachusetts

Acknowledgments

The Child's World®: Mary Berendes, Publishing Director

Editorial Directions, Inc.: E. Russell Primm, Editorial Director and Project Manager;
Katie Marsico, Associate Editor; Judith Shiffer, Assistant Editor; Caroline Wood, Editorial Assistant

The Design Lab: Kathleen Petelinsek, Design and Art Production

Library of Congress Cataloging-in-Publication Data

Simon, Charnan.
  My mother is a doctor / written by Charnan Simon ; illustrated by Patrick Girouard.
    p. cm. —(Magic door to learning)
  ISBN 1-59296-620-9 (library bound : alk. paper)
  1. Physicians—Juvenile literature. 2. Children—Preparation for medical care—Juvenile literature.
I. Title. II. Series.
  R690.S527 2007
  610.69'5—dc22   2006001411

A book is a door, a magic door.
It can take you places
you have never been before.
Ready? Set?
Turn the page.
Open the door.
Now it is time to explore.

My mother is a doctor.
She helps her patients heal.

A doctor listens carefully
to know just how you feel.

She looks inside your ears and mouth.

She listens to your heart.

She feels your
neck and tummy—
oops! That's the
ticklish part!

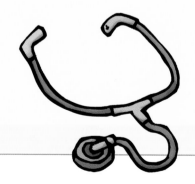

My mother has an
office. She works
in a hospital, too.

She helps you if
you break your arm
and when you get
the flu.

Sometimes she says, "Take these pills."

Sometimes she says, "Rest."

And then she
says, "You're doing
great!" That's what
she likes the best!

Our story is over, but there is still much to explore beyond the magic door!

Did you know that you can help your doctor? Doctors treat patients who are sick, but they also give people advice on how to stay healthy. Eating healthy foods is one great way to make sure you're in good shape the next time you see your doctor. Plan a special meal with your family. Have each person pick a food that should be part of your diet. Some foods to include are vegetables, fruits, low-fat cheese, and whole-grain breads. At your family meal, have everyone say why they picked the food they did and how it helps keep them healthy.

This book will help you explore at the library and at home:
Boyd, Nicole. *A Doctor's Busy Day*. New York: Rosen, 2002.

About the Author
Charnan Simon lives in Madison, Wisconsin, where she can usually be found sitting at her desk and writing books, unless she is sitting at her desk and looking out the window. Charnan has one husband, two daughters, and two very helpful cats.

About the Illustrator
Patrick Girouard broke his arm when he was three. One night, his parents found him trying to remove the cast with a butter knife! They thought he might become a doctor, but it was his sister Susan who did that, and everyone is very proud of her. Patrick lives in Indiana and has regular checkups.